The Quest For The Perfect Topping

Regan Vehrs

Copyright © 2024 by Regan Vehrs
All rights reserved. This book or any portion there of may not be reproduced or used in any manner whatsoever without the express written permission of the publisher except for the use of brief quotations in a book review.

DEDICATION

To Dad,

For always encouraging me to be my true self and for believing in me no matter what. Your love and support have given me the courage to embrace my uniqueness. Thank you for being my teacher, biggest fan, and constant source of inspiration, with all my love.

DEDICATION

To my Momma,

In a world full of mirrors and reflections, your true magic lies far beyond what we see. Your magic lies in your ability to turn ordinary moments into extraordinary memories, and your kindness sprinkles joy wherever you go.

Thank you for showing that true beauty is more than skin deep-it's in the kindness you show, the love you give, and the strength you share. You are the real magic in our story, making every day a little brighter and every moment a little more special.

To the radiant souls who shine from within, you are the sparkle in the stardust may you discover the boundless magic that lives within you.

With all my love,
Regan

In the bustling town of Sweetville, where sugar swirls in the air and the scent of freshly baked treats dances in the breeze, you can find a Cupcakery, a delightful shop known for its delectable cupcakes.

Rumor has it that these cupcakes are made with a magical touch, and once the 'open' sign is flipped to 'closed,' they come to life...

In the Sugar Kingdom, a little cupcake named Cherry from the Frosted Forest felt troubled. She felt somewhat uneasy because she lacked a special quality. Cherry strolled down the soft, pillowy streets of Frosted Forrest, wondering how to find the perfect topping.

She couldn't help but feel ordinary for not having any toppings. She often wished to stand out like the other cupcakes, thinking, "If only I could be like them." She wanted to feel like the best dressed in town.

Poof! Out of nowhere, a colorful and sparkling cupcake popped out of thin air before Cherry's eyes! The cupcake was sensational, with exciting sprinkles and candies. The cupcake's name was Sparkles, and Sparkles was summoned to help a fellow cupcake in need.

As Cherry's Sugary Godmother, Sparkles sensed Cherry's desire to find the perfect topping. With twinkling eyes and a kind smile, Sparkles whisked a sprinkle of fairy dust, and they were on their way.

They followed the Rocky Road trail to Chocolate Fudge Hills, a village made from chocolate. Bonbon Mountains lay across the horizon, and a river of fudge shimmers. Even the air was rich and heavenly. Across the river, Cherry spotted Cocoa Cupcakes with effortless chocolate toppings.

Cherry dressed in high chocolate fashion but didn't feel like it suited her. While beautiful in their own way, the drizzles were far too sticky for Cherry!

Cherry was not about to give up we're just getting started! Sparkles and Cherry crossed the Twizzler Bridge into Strawberry Fields, the land of all things pink!

There were rows of strawberries, a town made of angel food cake, and a strawberry milk waterfall in the cotton candy forest. Cherry couldn't wait to try on a strawberry topper. She just knew that it would be perfect for her!

21

As they entered Angel Town, Sparkles and Cherry were greeted by the friendliest cupcakes and were happy to see them! They explored the town and said hello to the townspeople, searching for the perfect strawberry.

It was time. Sparkles scaled the tall ladder to place the 'berry' heavy strawberry on top of Cherry's head. Cherry was giggling with anticipation.

To Cherry's disappointment, this topping didn't feel 'just right.' Despite the enchanting Strawberry Hills, the strawberry was far too heavy! The other cupcakes carry it flawlessly, and she felt discouraged.

Sparkles sensed her sadness growing and reminded her to remain optimistic and motivated to find the perfect one. Not to worry, she said, there was one more land to be discovered! Cherry's topping had to be there!

In a banana split boat, Cherry and Sparkles crossed the Strawberry Milk River to reach the land of Milk and Cookies—a castle made of ice cream and waffle cones beyond Marshmallow Meadow.

A magical sight lay before their eyes. This was the heart of Sweetville—different candies, sprinkles, gumdrops, sugar cones, graham crackers, and more covered the land!

There were so many options; how would she decide which was right?

Cherry tried on at least a dozen toppings, but no matter how many she tried, none seemed right! She felt out of place. Frustrated and disheartened, Cherry lost hope of finding what she was looking for.

35

Cherry decided it was time to return to the Frosted Forest. On their journey home, Sprinkles talked about their adventure. They had encountered a host of colorful characters on their journey, each special in their own unique way, and each land made them feel welcomed.

Sprinkles told Cherry that there is no such thing as a 'perfect topping' and that each cupcake's genuine sweetness comes not just from the ingredients or toppings but also from the love, kindness, and joy they have on the inside.

Cherry remembers the cupcakes she had met along their journey. She realizes that every cupcake she sees is special in its own unique way. It's not about having the most beautiful toppings or the fanciest decorations—true specialness comes from one's unique strengths and sharing kindness with others.

With this, Cherry returns to Frosted Forrest with a heart full of appreciation for the extraordinary qualities in herself and others. She admires the braveness, courage, curiosity, and creativity it took on her voyage with her Sugary Godmother by her side. She finally discovers that the true magic of Sweetville lies in the diversity and uniqueness of each cupcake that lives there -- Cherry being very much included.

www.ingramcontent.com/pod-product-compliance
Lightning Source LLC
LaVergne TN
LVHW071659060526
838201LV00037B/381